Time to play shops

A tribute to the WI Country Markets

Pictures and text by Jo Major

The Lutterworth Press Ⓛ

Published by
The Lutterworth Press
P.O. Box 60
Cambridge
CB1 2NT
England

e-mail: **publishing@lutterworth.com**
website: **http://www.lutterworth.com**

ISBN 0 7188 3044 X

British Library Cataloguing in Publication Data:
A catalogue record is available from the British Library.

First published by the Lutterworth Press 2004

Copyright © 2004, Jo Major

All rights reserved. No part of this publication may be reproduced, stored in a retrieval system or transmitted in any form or by any means, electronic, mechanical, photocopying, recording or otherwise, without prior written permission from the Publisher.

Printed in the People's Republic of China

Front cover: The Lesser Hall, Cowbridge, Glamorgan
Back cover: The Monteagle Community Hall, Yateley, Hampshire

1. An Introduction

Some time in the early summer of the year 2000 my mother asked me to accompany her on the local WI Market's annual outing. With my recently acquired status of student photographer in mind, I felt that such homely pursuits might be slightly beneath me and I was a little reluctant to accept. That September, however, I found myself beside her, on the coach hired for the day by the WI Market's Harleston branch in South Norfolk. Later that afternoon, whilst enjoying the hospitality of a neighbouring market's village hall tea, I sat next to Judy Forbes, chairman of the Harleston branch and listened to a story unfold that still astonishes me.

The £11 million turnover etc. . . .

All that summer I had been looking for a photographic project with which to complete my MA degree. That damp September day, travelling the quiet, rural lanes of my own East Anglia, I felt confident that I had found it.

I knew nothing at the time of the WI Markets, but within days I had found a turnover of £11 million, 510 branches, and 44,000 shareholders, each with a 5p share. I had also uncovered the fact that no thesis on this extraordinary organisation, photographic or otherwise, had ever been produced. Later that week, at 7.30 in the morning, I was at the doors of the Harleston branch weekly market, camera at the ready. The sight that greeted me as I pulled back the heavy curtain lifted my heart and flooded my senses. Produce still damp with the morning dew, fresh cakes, pies and pastries glistening beneath crisp Cellophane, flowery aprons whizzing back and forth and a row of café tables standing expectantly to one side; each one with a small vase of fresh flowers in the centre, thrown into relief in shafts of morning sunlight.

The village hall itself, where this phenomenon was taking place, stirred my childhood memories of draughty village halls and their local institutions. But this was no floundering activity, reliant on little more than a few die-hard loyalists. This was a modern organisation going like a steam train. That is to say, fast enough, with character, steady reliability and an uncomplicated confidence that what they do, they do better than anyone. These people were not just stallholders, not just workers; they were cooks and crafters; growers and busy 'grafters'. They seemed part of a crusade that had less to do with the Women's Institute's *Jerusalem* and everything to do with enjoying their day and being an energetic part of their small rural communities.

The WI Country Markets, *not* the Women's Institute

In contrast to their former parent group (The National Federation of Women's Institutes) the WI Country Markets are not a charity. Since 1916 when the first markets became the practical side of the Women's Institute movement they have been a thriving retail business. In 1995 the national organisation became a limited company in its own right, although still dedicated to the promotion of traditional home skills. In 2004 all formal ties with the NFWI ceased and the Markets began trading, with that £11 million turnover, under their new name, Country Markets.

Ninety percent of the turnover goes to the producers; of the 44,000 shareholders at least 13,000 produce goods in their home, small-holding or garden. For 5p anyone can become a shareholder. Anyone, anywhere can start a new branch and there is even a bursary of £100 with which to do it. Markets are closely regulated by health and safety standards and heavily patronised by both consumers and producers. Most products are made only a few miles from the market stall; you will probably buy them from their maker or grower. Every week people give their time freely, sharing the duties. The most popular produce is usually completely sold out within the first hour. In many markets the public queue to get in, then share local gossip over coffee and biscuits before they leave. At this grass-roots level of marketing, with the minimum of packaging, the complete absence of the usual goods distribution circus, and with great personal integrity, the produce and commitment is in a class of its own. Without government subsidy, this enduring and endearing cultural institution is a true co-operative in a capitalist society; a rare jewel indeed.

Identity, community, culture

The market's venues; village halls, disused corn exchanges, pubs, labour clubs, restored stables and community centres hold Britain's domestic history. The pictures, I hope, will provide a visual context for the reader to explore or revisit this part of the British rural way of life. But, in spite of their place in history this story is no pastoral elegy. This book is about a body of people with a coherent sense of identity at a time when personal and collective responsibility is considered to be in crisis. The Markets endorse community life when this is more often viewed as fragmenting. It depicts a powerful and effective display of culture in places that the tourist rarely sees. At a time when many of us want fairness, value and a more controllable way of life, the markets can be seen practicing all of these things; today and for the best part of the last century.

My book celebrates all aspects of this culture, a culture, in recent years, overshadowed by the rise of giant retailers and global consumerism. Shopping malls and high streets, where the corporate image rules, no longer satisfy all customers. Regional differences, local culture and identifiable, friendly faces are the shopper's new Holy Grail. The WI Markets, with their unique mix of flowery tablecloths, summer outings and solid economics, blend corporate identity with homely traditions; a mix of viable retailing, home-made pastry and plenty of fun.

The WI Markets' achievement

The serious nature of this enterprise also attracted me. Sometime in the future, the British people may well see these early hours of the 21st century as a defining moment, not just in the way they shop, but on the grander historical scale of personal and national identity. There is already lively interest and debate – how and where we produce our food; what we do with our leisure time; how small communities get together and what is important to them? As we strive to absorb and integrate other cultures that have made their homes here, the British identity, flourishing in all corners of the British Isles still demands attention. The WI Country Markets uphold this identity in 500 such corners of British towns and villages. The following pages are an entertaining and affectionate appraisal of this significant, yet unselfconscious achievement.

Since I began my research in 2000 there have been many changes within the markets, most internal. But one major change has coincided with this book – the WI Markets have changed their name. At the request of the NFWI they dropped the 'WI' initials from their corporate and trading names, a real watershed after 85 years of trading, and 10 years as a company. They now face an autonomous future previously unknown to them. My reason for writing this book stems from the juxtaposition of their historic connection with the Women's Institutes and their place in retailing today. The new name, Country Markets Ltd., has yet to figure in the public consciousness so I refer to them as the WI Markets.

Alongside the pictures and in a few chapters I offer some idea of the background, aspirations and human stories behind the markets. I cover different categories of interest: history and structure; produce; services and venues; financial facts. Each category has an interview and photographs of a shareholder. I end with a broad outline on how readers might start new Country Markets for themselves. So, if there is a branch near you then go there. If not then start one. Either way, simply enjoy the book.

Jo Major
October, 2004

2. The History

Their place in history

Following the trail of a well-known and well-documented institution back to its beginnings should be easy, a piece of cake you might say. But pinning the exact origins of the WI Markets down has been, at times, a slippery undertaking. Somewhere between the craggy gorse mounds of Anglesey and the stylish shopping baskets of Sussex I have unearthed the hard fact that the WI Country Markets *Limited* did not exist until 1995. This is because at that time, as remains the case today, workers within a charity could not take any personal profit, and the National Federation of Women's Institutes, which spawned the markets as long ago as 1916, is a charity. So in 1995, after much soul searching and table thumping and wringing of hands, the markets began operating as a separate organisation – a fully fledged limited company. In that year, and in spite of the WI Markets voting to keep the name 'WI', the National Federation of Women's Institutes and the WI Country Markets parted company. To quote a member of the national council at the time, *"our hands are still linked, but at arm's length"*. Regardless of this mutually agreed separation there is an NFWI representative on the Market's board of directors; changes to any of the Market's rules and regulations must be approved by the NFWI and, of course, some of the markets still have people who belong to the NFWI. Well, quite a few do, er . . . nearly all of them, actually. Nevertheless, the history of The WI Country Markets *Limited* begins in 1995. Did they, then, begin in the early or the late twentieth century, and where does all this history and tradition come into it, if at all? Where, exactly, was the first WI Market? You may not be surprised to know that, to this question, there is no simple answer.

First of all, it all depends on whether you want to include this pre-1995 affiliation with the Women's Institutes or not. This is to say, the WI of risqué-calendar fame; the WI of putting self-seeking-prime-ministers-in-their-place fame; the WI who brought about the demise of turnstiles in public loos, and championed the Keep-Britain-Tidy campaign; the WI who helped bring running water and electricity to many outlying rural communities. In other words, the WI which has worked tirelessly to improve the lives of country people, an achievement not unfamiliar to many WI Market producers of today. You would, however, be invited by many of the current shareholders to view their organisation in the light of being a thriving *new* business that only just pre-dates the Farmer's Markets, which began in 1997, and has no connection whatever with the NFWI other than using the name for the past ten years. But to do this you would be missing the great pool of activity that has shaped the WI Markets and nurtured their unique place in our history. A uniqueness that firmly sets them apart from any other straightforward table top retailing, market style or otherwise. If then your perspective on their history is to include the NFWI itself, to find the original market you must choose between 'official' WI history and the facts. Confused? Well, let's start again.

Ontario, Criccieth, Lewes and The Carnegie Trust

To get a true perspective of the entire bun-fight we must go right back to the 1890s, to a place called Stoney Creek, in Ontario in Canada, where the work of the Women's Institute began. Shortly before the First World War, in 1913, Mrs Alfred Watt, a renowned Canadian speaker on the rights of country women, brought the newly formed idea of the Institutes to Britain. Three years later it took root in Anglesey, at Llanfair PG (that's the Llanfair with the indescribably long name to you and me) That same year, 1916, and not too far down the road at Criccieth in Caernavon, Mrs Dorothy Drage, a staunch supporter of Mrs Watt, formed the Criccieth Women's Institute. This was during the German U-boat blockade of the Atlantic in the First World War. A result of this was the wartime government's warning that within three weeks the country would run out of food. In answer to this warning Mrs Drage became part of a successful endeavour to encourage the production and distribution of locally grown produce. As a founding member of the WI she would have been keen to uphold the early 'Objects of the Institutes' as published in 1916 by Mrs Watt. These objectives included the following; *1) Studying home economies. 2) Providing centres for educational and social intercourse. 3) Encouraging home and local industries.* And, most significantly, *4) Developing co-operative enterprises* In keeping with this newly formed manifesto of improving country life, Mrs Drage organised the distribution of food as part of the WI work to which she was committed. This distribution took the guise of a market run as a co-operative, in the WI room, on the outskirts of the town. This room was a little wooden Drill Hall donated by Mrs Drage's family. A hall (page 11) still stands on the site. The following is an extract from Mrs Drage's autobiography *Pennies for Friendship*

A sale was held twice a week in the Women's Institute room by voluntary workers. Goods were sold wholesale to the trade till 4pm after which retail sales finished the day. . . . We took turns in collecting and selling. We had anxious moments on several days, wondering how much produce was going to come in, and welcomed with joy the larger amounts from the large gardens and farms, as our sales included eggs as well as vegetables and fruit. This work was done by the co-operative society of members who were profiting by the collection and sale of foodstuffs. . . . We proceeded from marketing activities by ourselves, with the help of the A.O.S. [Agricultural Organisation Society, a government department and forerunner of today's DEFRA] *in forming a registered co-operative association of the WI and its producers.*

The British shopkeeper spirit blossomed and within a few months five more markets had sprung up around Caernavon. Unfortunately their success was their downfall and pressure from jealous and suspicious local traders was brought to bear. By 1927 they had all closed. Meanwhile, in 1919, in Lewes, Sussex, and for much the same reasons as Criccieth, that is to help the distribution of local food, another WI market had begun. Because it has traded almost continuously to this day it is this market that 'official' WI history marks as the very first of the present organisation. And there you have it, that is, of course, unless you want to stick with the 1995 contingent. In truth, if you want to be 'bib and braces' about where the first market took place, you will have to choose between whose bib and which brace came first for yourself. Personally, I'm with Mrs Drage.

For many participants, past and present, in the Markets their place in history is about achievement, not dates. The Markets and the National Federation of Women's Institutes like it or not, are still, in spirit at least, joined at the hip. They have shared nearly a century of service to the community through self help and organised effort. This has included formal training in bottling and canning, an egg-collecting depot and the formation of a 'Guild of Learning' for home crafts. It embraced government backed production and distribution of jam during World War Two, and perhaps most important of all, an ever-present quest to provide opportunity and self confidence to those whose horizons might have been otherwise limited. From 1916, in a little wooden drill hall, to the present day in nearly 500 branches, their pretty and productive tabletops have been the public face of the Women's Institute. Their reasons for divorce have stemmed from one thing only; paying tax. The National Federation formed itself, quite rightly, into a charity to avoid it; the markets became an independent co-operative so that they could, where necessary, pay it. This time it really is that simple, and there is even a date with which to pin it down.

Throughout the First World War and the 1920s the markets had been largely a hit and miss affair, often referred to as "The WI market stalls" or simply "the stalls". But in 1932, in the same year as a generous donation of £1,000 from the Carnegie UK Trust (of Carnegie Hall fame), a conference changed the future of the markets. So as not to compromise the WI's status as a charity, the markets became an independent co-operative, and the first handbook was published (see page 10).

The controlling hand of the WI had not disappeared; it had merely retreated to the paperwork. An extract from the first handbook compiled by Vera Cox, the Marketing Organiser, (page 2, section 3) reads:

In order to meet the national need for the organisation of supplies from small producers, those starting marketing undertakings should be encouraged to organise stalls on as wide a basis as possible, serving not only Women's Institute members but also other small producers in their district. . . . The voluntary service which Women's Institute members are so ready to give will be necessary as before, and it is believed that the members will carry into this new venture the spirit of co-operation which the Institutes have fostered.

These suggestions from the handbook are still being followed, to the letter. The Carnegie Trust continued to monitor the development of the markets for years, as an extract from their Annual Report for 1934 shows:

The experiment in co-operative rural marketing, promoted by the National federation of Women's Institutes, towards the cost of which the Trustees have decided to make a further grant of £500 a year for the three years 1935, 1936, 1937, has continued to yield valuable lessons. It has been supervised by a special committee, with an expert organiser, composed partly of Women's Institute members and partly of representatives of the Ministry of Agriculture and the County Councils Association. Societies are advised to register under the Industrial and provident Societies act, and to conform to a set of rules approved by the Registrar of Friendly Societies. They are not limited to Women's Institute members; they admit small producers generally, including unemployed allotment holders. Markets (which numbered 69 by September 1934) may be either small wayside stalls open only from time to time in the summer, or larger markets served by a group of villages and open once or twice a week throughout the year. A recent calculation showed a turnover of £27,563, of which £25,517 had been paid to producers. It is stated that already there is a marked improvement in the quality and appearance of produce; this is partly due to teaching given in local schools arranged in conjunction with the Ministry and county councils. So far development has been mainly in the South and West of England, and it may be that different methods are necessary in the North and in Scotland. The Federation have undertaken to investigate this problem in the near future.

The WI's brand of co-operative marketing never did reach Scotland, but the ethos was firmly planted at this time in England and Wales and feverishly endorsed by The Carnegie UK Trust. Co-operatives, big and small, are still an important part of our retailing experience today. In 1995, the year the limited company became a reality, the ICA (Independent Co-operative Association) Centennial Congress, held in Manchester, adopted the following statement on the 'Co-operative identity':

Definition: *A co-operative is an autonomous association of persons united voluntarily to meet their common, economic, social and cultural needs and aspirations through a jointly owned and democratically controlled enterprise.*
Values: *Co-operatives are based on the*

The Llanfair PG Women's Institute Hall, on Anglesey, where the first regular meetings of the Institute were held. It is still used for Institute meetings today.

Mrs Dorothy Drage, pictured in her garden at Bron Eifion, Anglesey, where the first meeting of the Women's Institute was held. She organised the first WI markets in Britain. They were Caernavon, Criccieth, Pwllheli, Llanfarfechan, Portmadoc, and Llanbedr. By 1927, they had all closed.

Site of the Drill Hall in Criccieth, where the first market was held in 1916. It belonged to the family of Dorothy Drage, and was donated, for the good of the community, to the newly formed Institute. The present-day hut is used by the Scouts.

values of self-help, self-responsibility, democracy, equality, equity and solidarity. In the tradition of their founders, co-operative members believe in the ethical values of honesty, openness, social responsibility and caring for others.

Few other organisations can claim to uphold this statement with as much integrity and enthusiasm as the WI Markets.

So much for the history, but what of today, and what of the future, a future without wearing the WI initials like a well trusted makeup? Today, as in the future, they stand as they have always stood, un-fazed by history, a heart in their small communities beating on despite the turbulence around. Culture could, indeed, be described as a steady beating heart.

Their place in their culture

The organic process in a country or community, producing an identifiable culture is hardly noticeable until it has gone. A re-creation of that culture then becomes inevitable. A rise in the, often commercially driven, 'heritage' culture begins to take the place of the original, often as little more than pastiche. Britain is peppered with such 'heritage' sites. They are successful on only one level, as a record. They do not progress other than to collect dust. The WI weekly markets are the antithesis of this sorry process. By contrast, they evolve and change continuously against a backdrop of local history, national history and the events of the wider world. The result is a living culture, bottled and preserved, as surely as their jam, within their everyday tasks and their simple surroundings.

It is this richness of culture that has struck me with such force in my visits to the markets around the UK. Small details speak volumes to the inquisitive eye looking for evidence of a lively and natural identity. A wall clock or a notice board in a village hall; the print of tablecloth, the cut of an apron or the design of a chair; a fading picture of the Queen's young children, Charles and Anne hanging on the wall.

These are details that if lingered over for too long dissolve into individual memories. Collectively they become marks of identity and culture. The artless use of the ordinary and the everyday can render a culture indestructible. This is the achievement of the WI Markets and similar organisations. A little of the 'pastiche' may sometimes slip in, such as the ladies of Holsworthy in Devon wearing their straw boaters. But in such earnest surroundings it feels right, is completely harmless and adds a frisson of cheeky humour. (Sorry Holsworthy, no offence meant.)

Their place in their community

The people of the markets would of course, question that their place in history should be couched in such grand and noble terms. They are much more concerned with their place in the high street or the town's market car park. This, they would say, is where the seat of their activity and commerce really lies. Such common sense cannot be ignored. What is important to them is that their physical presence in their community is visible, accessible and works for them. Brampton Market in Cumbria performs weekly in an imposing little building slap in the middle of a busy outdoor market. It rises proudly from a sea of tented stalls like a giant prop, centre stage. Princes Risborough Market in Buckinghamshire integrates with locals effortlessly, out in the open, right by the town's main bus stop. (I do not mean to say that standing in the open for four hours a week directly in the path of the north wind is effortless, merely productive in terms of bagging shoppers.) These considerations come first. The interaction between marketeer and customer, that forms such a valuable part of this life, is not going to happen if they can't find each other.

So how is it that Pwllheli (say Poofhelly) Market in Caernafon gets on so well tucked away down a back street, through a car park and into the *back* entrance of a dismal council building? The answer to this seeming contradiction is that retailing is only one part of the market's 'place' in its community. To find the other we must plunder the more opaque depths of theory in human behaviour. If, as a reader, all you want is a fun look at the WI Markets in action, then fast forward now. You will find all you need in the photographs. But if you want to know why markets like Pwllheli turn over enough money to keep twenty producers happy, then read on....

The Markets' place in retailing

A market is only a retail operation you might say. People go to buy 'stuff'. True, but much more goes on at a market, any market, than the mere exchange of money. What is available in a market, whether a Farmer's Market in a small town, the Portobello Road, London, on a busy summer Saturday, or the WI Market in a back street in Pwllheli, is community interaction. We go to look each other in the eye. We want to invest the exchange of money for goods with a personal value, an experience we can take away with us. It is one aspect that confounds the giant retailers looking on from their lofty positions in the outer limits of high finance and global consumerism. Try as they might, they cannot package and sell this human need to interact. The very act of organising human activity will almost certainly bring about a silence as people wait to be told what to do. The closest a supermarket might get is in its café, but even here the only spontaneous interaction is likely to be in the queue at the till. To compare these 'conveyer belt' style cafés with the friendly chatter and table-hopping found at a WI Market's refreshment area is a helpful way to understand the basic difference in a public venue and a social event. The difference, if you like, between a stop-over and a destination. A WI Market, like other markets, is a sought-out destination, and whether in a busy square or tucked away down a country lane, succeeds where the supermarkets, in their sterile quest for profit, fail.

In contrast to the human interaction found in markets, forty years of supermarket culture have relentlessly fed a solitary individuality. The Shopper-with-the-purse is the star of this mass consumerism, and one of the icons in modern life. The almost insatiable desire to sell and consume has left us communicating in the most efficient way – wordlessly. Credit cards, club cards, catalogues and the Internet have woven a web of silence around everyday transactions. We often now make a phone call in silence, using only codes and numbers. Under such conditions, looking the other party in the eye feels like lost treasure. The market tradition leads us right back to that treasure.

Although the busiest branch of the WI Markets, Chichester, turns over nearly £80,000 a year there are branches that could be described as little more than a coffee morning. The movers and shakers of the organisation can only look on with benign tolerance, as they are obliged to support such an affair. But the value to an individual member of a community, producer, helper or customer, in such circumstances is the same as a large market keeping its queue at bay and needing two people to bank the money. Running a business is about money, but running a market taps into a much deeper need, the desire to be together. This is the cement that holds the WI Markets together.

To find anyone in a WI Market producing for the money alone is rare. There are exceptions, of course, particularly where commercial producers join, but they are outnumbered by those who want to get out of their homes to meet people, or to share their interests with others. The weekly helpers earn only a pat on the back and a thank you! In my own surveys I have discovered that out of the 44,000 shareholders, only 13,000 produce goods and only 7,000 act as helpers. The remaining 24,000, along with the many non-shareholders who shop there, merely use the markets. They turn up each week to buy the produce, meet their neighbours or simply for the regular, enjoyable activity. Marry these fundamental needs to the love of cooking, gardening and making or organise, and a WI Market is likely to appear. This offers an improvement in people's lives, and is where the markets, regardless of the recent name change, still sit comfortably within the ethos of the National Federation of Women's Institutes, although both 'sides' will loudly protest their autonomy. Such a happy mix of supply and demand creates activity anywhere: from a town square to a quiet village hall; from the back room of a pub to the platform of a railway station (Whitley Bay perform fortnightly to the backdrop of regular train services running through the station); from well-known to obscure places. Wherever there is a WI Market, it is there because it is wanted and needed. You can be confident that whatever is on offer is backed up by a solid and workable structure, formulated through almost a century of history. It is this structure that sets the WI Markets apart from any other retailing enterprise. It is the structure of a well-founded and far-reaching co-operative.

The AGM, 2001, Central Hall, Westminster

3. The Structure

The Market Branches

The structure of the WI Markets is an effective, democratic network of co-operative power; a network reaching from the table top in the market branch, to the top table of the board of directors. Everyone has a chance; everyone has a voice. It works like this: every market branch is run entirely by shareholders, each with a 5p share and a vote within their local market. This forms the base of the cooperative. The shares entitles them to sell produce at their own weekly market, to help with the duties and to take part in the branch management committee, meeting at least monthly. The member may be elected as Chairman, Secretary, Controller or Treasurer, or to attend an AGM., at county or national level, or as a Market Adviser (MA). There are approximately 500 market branches.

The County Societies

The County Market Society, of which the shareholder is a co-owner, is at the halfway point in the cooperative, with its AGM open to all members. A management committee keeps the share register up to date and produces audited accounts for all its branches. It has representatives from each branch in the county, a representative from the National Federation of Women's Institutes (NFWI) and one or more Market Advisers. They meet quarterly to discuss the well-being of the individual markets, hear news from the NFWI, and accept, or reject, new shareholders. The 81 County Market Societies are governed by the Financial Services Act (incorporating the 'Industrial Provident and Friendly Societies'), which provides guidance and regulations for trading.

The National Limited Company

The County Market Society in turn, has shares in the national organisation, WI Country Markets Ltd, now renamed as Country Markets Ltd. These shares enable the county market societies to send a delegate to the national AGM with a vote and to elect their board of directors. Country Markets Ltd acts as a national management committee, educating, training and providing a national link between the shareholders and other organisations. It holds databases of everything from legal matters to suppliers; from national policy to publicity. The company appoints a Market Adviser, recommended by the County Society. Six directors, elected at the AGM by the county societies, can serve three two-year periods.

The Co-operative with the Corporate Structure

Most positions in the market organisation are held for two years, which helps regenerate ideas, and has kept the markets buoyant and progressive, whilst retaining their strong traditions. In contrast to the NFWI, who have in the past taken extra care to present themselves to the outside world as part of the *un*-changing face of Britain, the WI Markets have change built into their very structure. As a result they are in a constant healthy state of flux, completely in tune with modern retailing. Within each market change is a constant force with a regular turnaround of people in charge. Outside influence also brings about change as venues open, close and move all the time, according to local supply and demand. The clever design of this fluid corporate structure underpins an unbroken chain of interests, from the customer at the market table to the bureaucrat at the European Commission. This process is refreshingly free of any other personal or corporate motives, such as shareholder's dividends, employee's salaries or the often stringent demands imposed upon a charity. There are precious few organisations that can make such a claim. This structure was, of course, fostered by the Women's Institute itself, which developed the National Federation concept as a pro-active tool for activities, and who still use it effectively today. But it is the WI Markets who have taken this concept out into the market place where they have watched it flourish. Such a network could be a blueprint to operate any business or organisation as a co-operative that works; that CO-operates, where the chairman of the board is just as likely to be baking a jam sponge for the market as to be arranging to meet an MP.

4. The Cooks

In any one year the Markets' cooks bake more than three million kilos of flour, fat and sugar. The cooks must hold a Basic Food Handling Hygiene Certificate. Their own shareholders handbook states: *"No produce should ever be sold in a WI market unless it is home-produced by the shareholder. It must be absolutely fresh and of good quality."* This means no ready-made pastry or fillings. It also points out that kitchens and transport must be pet and laundry free; that raw and cooked food must not occupy the same vicinity; cooks must wear protective clothing and not smoke while handling food or where it is stored, and must not cook if they are unwell or tired. These stringent standards apply to the food labelling, production, storage, transport and point of sale. Their motto is: **"Sell the best – eat the rest"**

The Lesser Hall, Cowbridge, Vale of Glamorgan

Clockwise from bottom left: Lincoln, Evesham, Yateley, Eden Valley, Eden Valley

Methodist Hall, Stokesley, North Yorkshire

Clockwise from bottom left: Melton Mowbray, Ludlow, Droitwich, Eden Valley, Wool

The Crown and Sceptre, Holsworthy, Devon

The Cooking

Audrey Jones [right and below right] has been at the centre of the WI markets on the Isle of Anglesey, home of the original Women's Institute in 1916, since 1974. She believes very strongly in the ethos of the WI movement, *"I've lived a lot of my life for the WI. This Jam and Jerusalem thing is always used out of context. Jam is a product but the words of Jerusalem are still the WI's collective voice."* Audrey is chairman for Wales NFWI But cooks unceasingly for the Llangefni Market. *"I never miss a week."*

Jill Graham [left and above] is helping her husband, a farmer in Gloucestershire, diversify from the stringent limitations of present-day farming. Jill bakes all day and every day; cottage pies, fish pies, beef and ale and steak and kidney. Lamb and asparagus, chicken pies and sausage rolls. Her speciality is Somerset pie made with pork, smoked bacon and leek, flavoured with cider and sage. She loves the customer interaction at her local WI market, Moreton-in-Marsh, and would never give it up. Jill has also been an NFWI member since the 1970s.

Peggy's Welsh cakes

Sieve together; 225g of self-raising flour, a teaspoon of mixed spice and a pinch of salt.
Rub in 115g of butter.
Add ; 80g of castor sugar, 115g of currants and a lightly beaten egg.
Mix with a fork to stiff dough.
Turn onto a lightly floured surface.
Roll out to a generous 5mm.
Cut into rounds with a 5cm fluted cutter.
Cook low on a griddle or a heavy frying pan for 5 minutes; turn for a further 2 minutes.
Cool and serve, sprinkled with castor sugar or spread with butter.

Peggy Knight cooks for the Isle of Portland Market in Dorset. She specialises in celebration cakes, and in iced floral decoration in particular. The flowers on the cake seen opposite are all made by hand from sugar. "*I enjoy baking and sugar-craft, and it pays for one of us to go on holiday.*" Another speciality are her simple Welsh cakes [see recipe], a legacy from her years living in Wales.

5. The Preserves

The Stables, Ruislip, Middlesex

A million pots of jam, marmalade, lemon curd, pickle and chutney are sold nationwide each year. Jams and marmalades must contain at least 60% sugar, known as the soluble solid content, to ensure a good set. The fruit used in them must be thoroughly washed, this includes the outer skins of citrus fruits for marmalade which uses the whole fruit. Although jars can be re-cycled, they must be fully sterilised and the lids must be brand new and drip-proof, with 'puff component lining'. To be sure of a good seal the jars are filled to the brim. Every jar is then labelled with the weight and the details of the producer. So if you buy jam from a WI Market, you can write and tell the person who made it (not just a faceless company) what you think.

The Metro Railway Station, Whitley Bay,
Tyne and Wear

Clockwise from bottom left:
Greet, Evesham, Lincoln, Marshalswick, Droitwich

The WI Hall, Bridport, Dorset

The Mayoress

Fiona Thwaytes making tomato jam from her mother's recipe, first published in 1933 (see opposite page). "*Baking for the markets does pay its way, although it's the tradition I enjoy.*" Her daughter, Annabelle, shops at the Eden Valley Market early every Friday to buy lemon cake, which she then sends to her two children away at university. Four generations, sixty years, one market and still going strong, their turnover last year; £13,000!

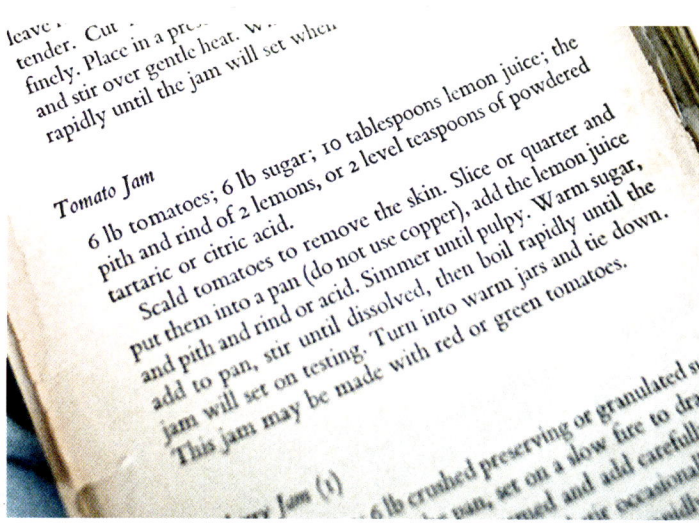

Fiona and her husband, Lancelot, serve their local community in many other ways: here Fiona proudly wears her chain of office as the Mayoress, in front of a portrait of her husband, the Mayor of Appleby-in-Westmoreland.

The Jam Class

Training can range from a branch controller's helpful hint to full residential courses at the NFWI's Denman college. A local jam class like this one at Yateley helps endorse the WI Markets' attention to detail and stringent quality control.

Ray Lush (below) helped his mother with her fruit preserving until her death in 1998. Since then he has kept her tradition going with a weekly supply of jams, marmalades, pickles and chutneys, all made to her recipes and the markets high standards . . . home-made or supermarket; jam doesn't come much better than this.

Although Bridget Norris (above right) is mainly a helper, she also sells greetings cards. (see above) She joined Yateley Market only a year ago.

I had my arm twisted by a friend to help out with a market parcel delivery, when I turned up at the market my eyes started wandering around and I thought to myself, hmmm, I can see my cards in here!

She then wanted to know everything about the WI Markets and joined a jam class organised by their controller, Marilyn Rogers. The sketch (right), which was her way of taking notes, shows her cheeky humour and her astonishing talent for cartoons.

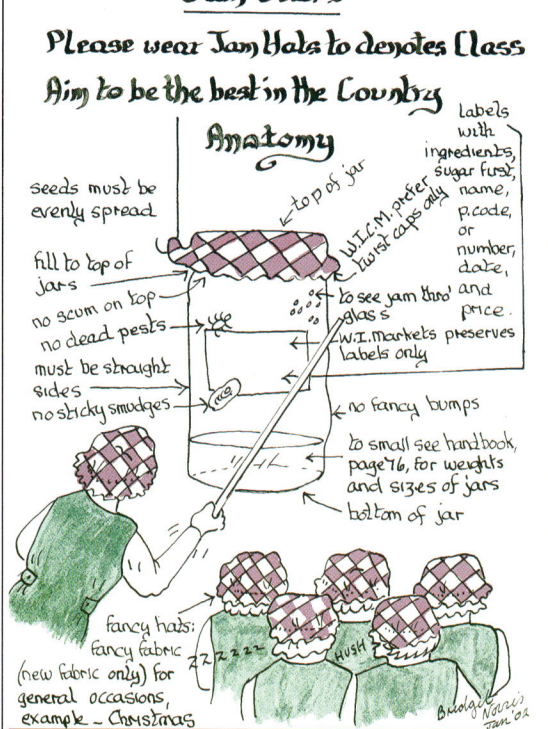

Mounteagle Community Hall, Yateley, Berkshire

Marmalade – all year round

Hilda's grandfather, brother and husband, Tim, were all farmers. Now she and Tim are involved in many local activities. They are still self-sufficient for vegetables and meat, and grow fresh produce for the market in their efficient set of tunnels. They both help at the weekly market every Wednesday, and, as can be seen on page 80, Hilda does her turn at the teapot. She also plays the church organ and has been a member of her Denton (Norfolk) branch of the Womens Institutes since 1955 when it began. It now has 30 active members and is still an important focal point for the village.

Hilda Thomas makes marmalade for Harleston market every day, using the best Sevilles whenever possible. She does not drive a car so all her ingredients come via her village shop, which she supports with a vengeance, although she will not buy vegetables grown out of season from anyone. Coming from a farming family, she feels very strongly about the stranglehold of the supermarkets over their suppliers. "I *never* use a supermarket, not ever, not for *anything*!"

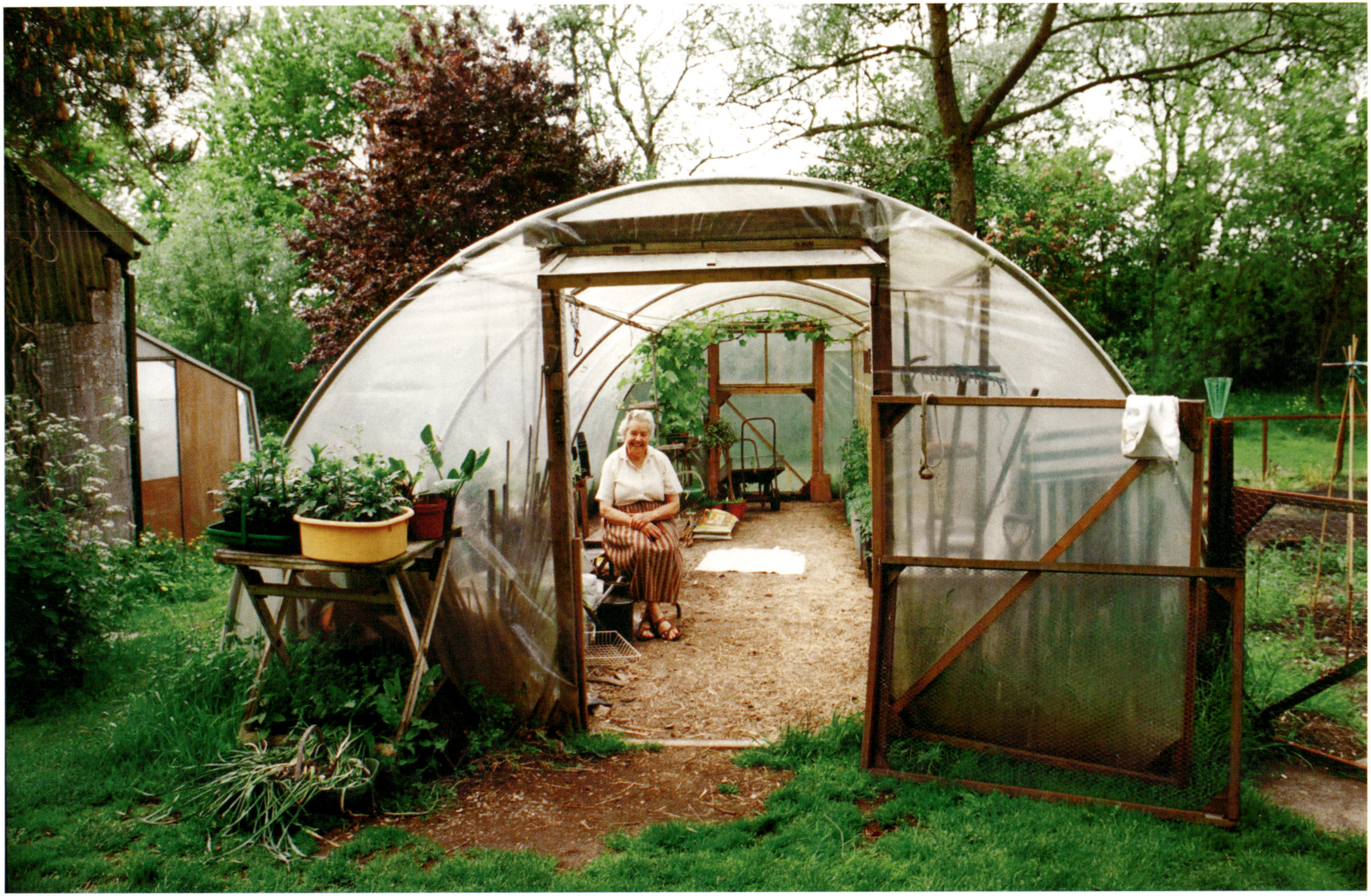

Trinity Methodist Church Hall, Hexham, Northumberland

6. The Growing

Clockwise from top left: Wool, Pwllheli, Chew Valley

The Market growers lead the field in fresh and organic produce from gardens or allotments. Commercial growers would not even try to compete at this modest level of output. Produced to the market's own standards, free of all chemical additives and carrying, where required, supporting DEFRA certificates to show growing conditions, the produce is harvested before it is fully mature and will be on the stall within hours of being picked or dug. Produce should be graded and clean; all packaging must be new and well ventilated. Each year the Markets will sell 1.1 million garden shrubs, pot-grown in sterile compost for at least four weeks, 620,000 vegetable and fruit plants, 500,000 kilos of fresh produce and 165,000 bunches of fresh and fragrant flowers, which will have been cut only a few hours before being sold from the table top.

The Old School, Long Melford, Suffolk

pages 44-45: The Corn Exchange, Helston, Cornwall

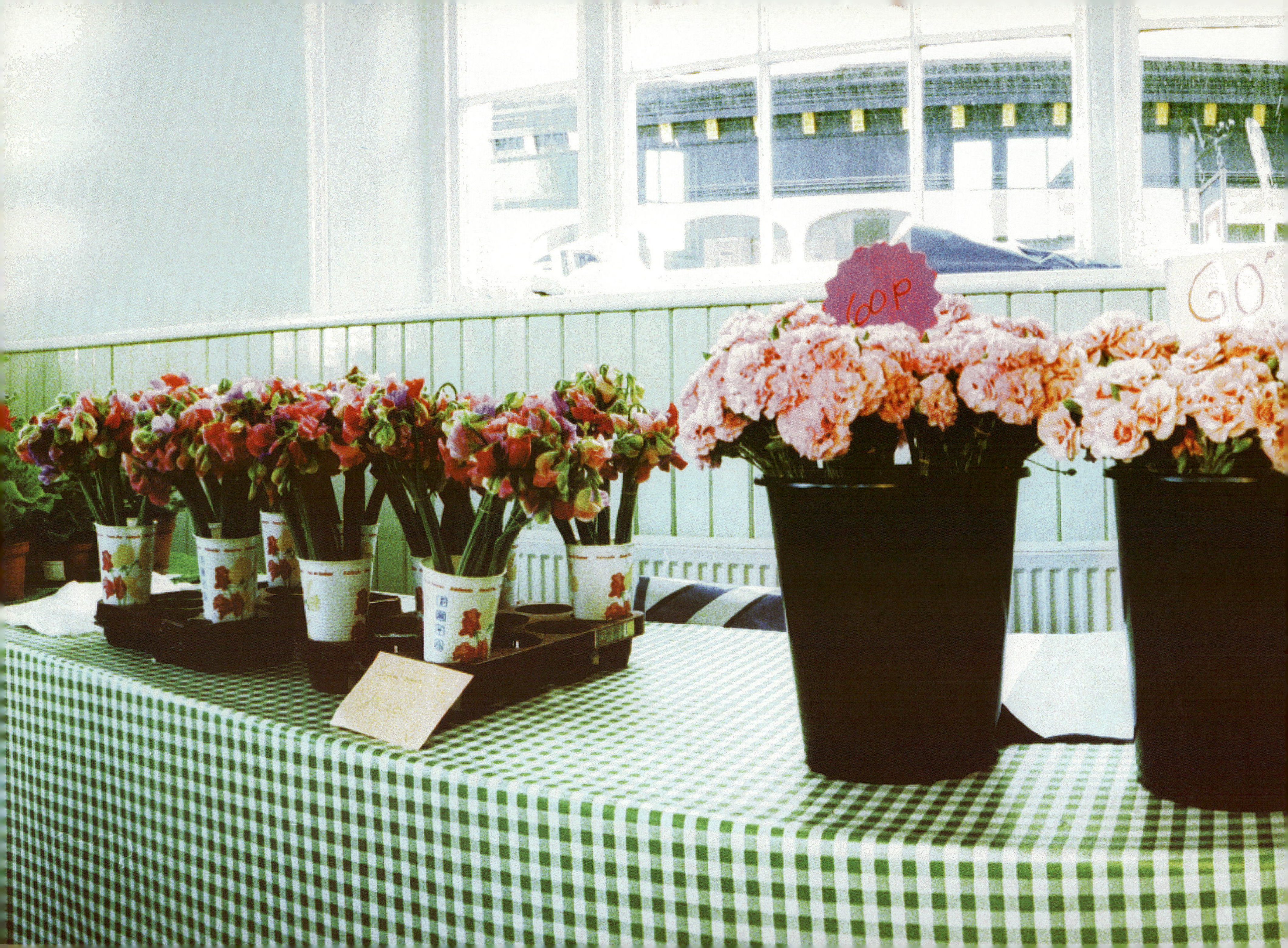
60P
60

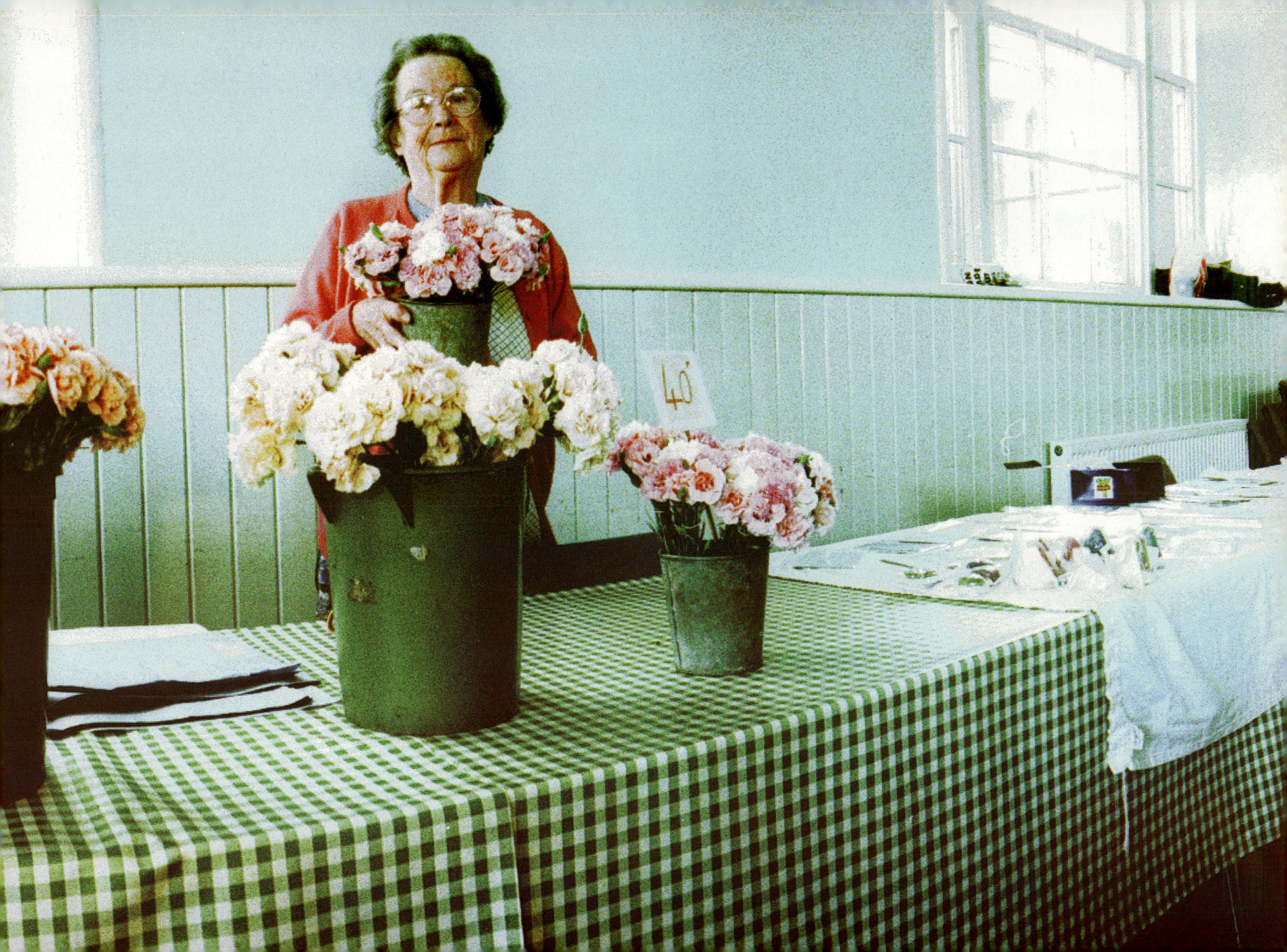
40

Clockwise from left:
Chew Valley, Backwell, Chapel St. Leonards, Portland

King George's Hall, Harleston, Norfolk

The Market Garden

The Channel Islands boasts a special place in the nation's growing of produce. This is borne out by the quality and the proliferation of Hilary Paul's vegetables and flowers. Healthy hours of sunshine, gentle winters and the fertile soil of Jersey are further enhanced by Hilary's dedication in collecting seaweed from a nearby bay as her favourite form of fertiliser. Hilary sells her produce at St Helier Market.

Hilary's green fingers have been growing fresh produce for the St Helier market since 1976. Her husband Harry sorts, picks, labels and does the sums. Harry has been prominent on Jersey since 1947, but Hilary traces her ancestry on the island back to 1648! Although she is not an NFWI member, her mother was and helped found an NFWI branch on Jersey in the 1960s.

John Stevenson and Charles Moss collecting beans for their local market (see page 47)

The Fruit Farm

The Craners also sell fruit at three Farmer's Markets in the area. Pam's husband, Michael, a grain trader, does nearly all this work as he knows most of the farmers, while Pam sees to the everyday running of the PYO, the shop and the WI. She also makes and sells jam regularly *"it's so easy, if it's not the best for selling, then into the pot it goes!"*

Pam Craner has run a successful 'Pick Your Own' (PYO) fruit farm in Essex for nearly twenty years, and is the major fruit supplier at both Hatfield and Hertford markets. *"I try not to swamp them if others bring in fruit. But when they run out they let me know and I'm there. It's all very friendly."*

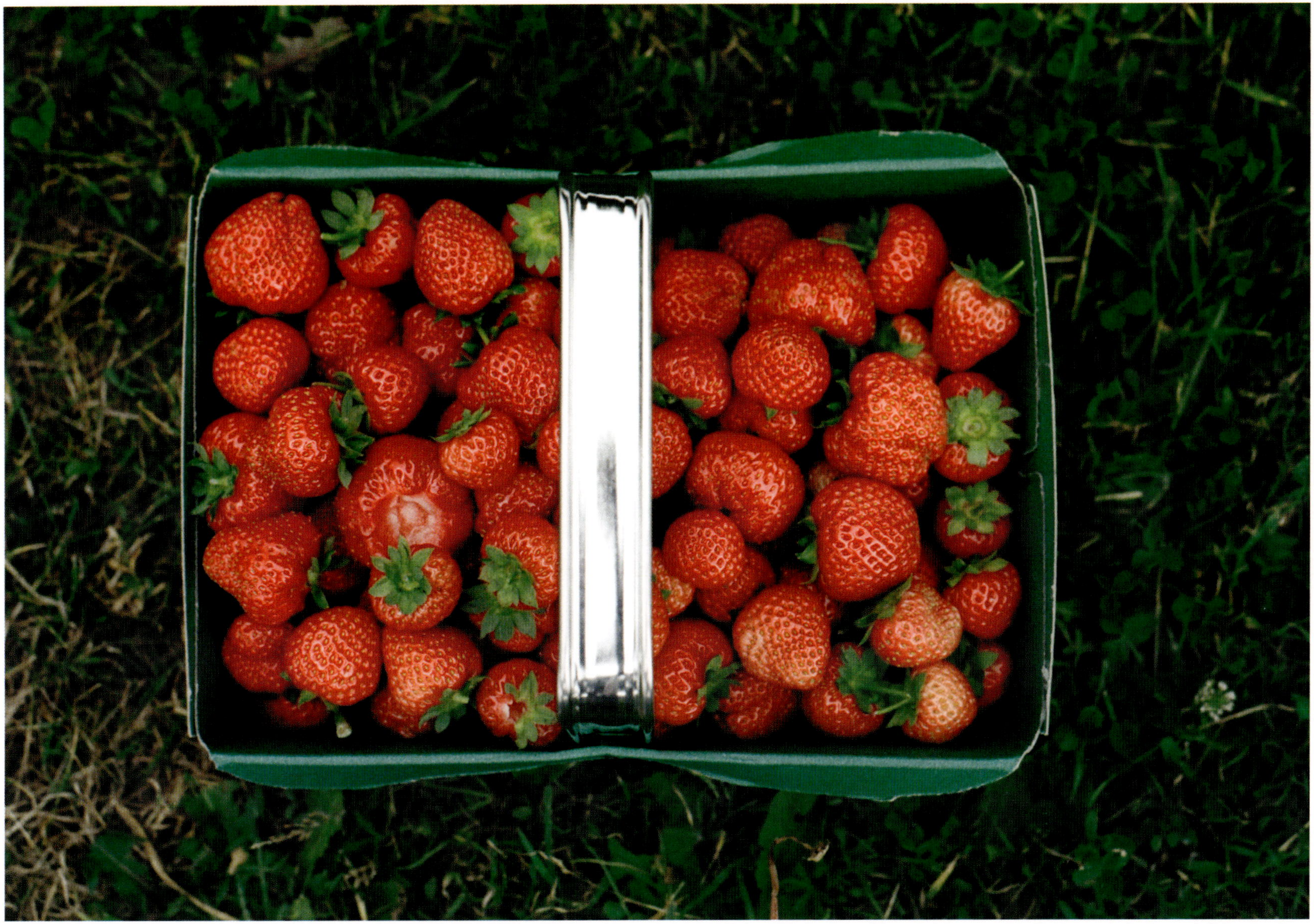

7. The Crafts

The Town Hall, Northallerton, North Yorkshire

Sewing, woodwork, pewter-work and knitting, jewellery, lace making, millinery and knitting, cane-chair repair and basketry, stained glass and glass engraving, china painting, pottery, patchwork, and knitting, hand-made cards and candles, framed pictures and more knitting. Knitted sweaters, hats and baby clothes are by far the most popular craft. *10,000 pairs of knitted baby bootees were sold last year.* A strict ratio of 75% skill from the shareholder to 25% raw material is applied, and each item must be made in its entirety by the shareholder. No kits are allowed and all materials must be new, not recycled. Modern, traditional and regional crafts with a high standard of skill and workmanship are encouraged. If an item does not sell after three months, then it will be withdrawn from sale.

Clockwise from bottom left:
Isle of Portland, St Helier, Dorchester, Conway, Clitheroe

56

Clockwise from bottom left:
Ludlow, Sherborne, Roseland, Charing, Greet

The Memorial Hall, Roseland, Cornwall

Clockwise from left:
Ware, Marshalswick, Clitheroe

The Women's Centre, Ludlow, Shropshire

The Craftworkers

Ill health has forced Bill Locke (right) out of work, so he started making walking sticks from hazel wood picked up in nearby woodland. He now produces all kinds of furniture, along with flower boxes, birdhouses and hanging baskets, from the nut wood. His wife, Hazel, who does exquisite Chinese brush paintings, introduced Bill to the market in Greet, where he is now a regular.

Diane Marks (left) only started working with tannelised wood to produce bird tables, garden pots and benches in 2003. She sells through a few local shops as well as Barnard Castle WI market. *"I'm a wood machinist but I go out and flog them as well, it's good fun"*

Michelle Giles (below and below left) does a fifty-minute drive twice each day to her work as a full time administrator for a water company. She began with the WI market five or six years ago as a way of unwinding. *"I enjoy being with the people at the market each week, it really helps me to relax."*

Michelle brings her needlecraft with her to the market every Saturday. But at home she gets involved with china painting, jewellery, cards, pressed flowers, water colours and finger painting. *"I flit from one thing to another, I just do what I enjoy, to get pleasure out of it. There's no pressure, I really like that."*

Derek Leach lives in West Bradford near Clitheroe, Lancashire. He has been working with wood for seven years, since his retirement as a building inspector. Wood turning is not new to him, as his first job was as an apprentice to a joiner. He sells his work at Clitheroe Market.

The Glass Room

Barbara Burgess has been producing works of art for the WI Market in Conway and Trefriw for twelve years. She also teaches stained-glass work, for 3 days a week, in colleges around the Conway area.

Barbara works in a small room adjacent to her home in the Vale of Conway. More and more she works with 'warm' glass which is kiln-fused. This gives her more products for the commercial market place, such as jewellery. For this method she needs a type of glass more easily available from the U.S. *"I'm always trying to produce new products, and this leads to needing new kinds of glass."* Barbara also supplies a few shops and sells at several craft fairs. *"It's just nice to get the products out there!"*

Barbara Burgess with a work commissioned for a new contemporary art gallery in Llanrwst

Vale Douzaine Room, Guernsey Vale, Channel Islands

8. The Grocery

Many markets sell honey, fresh meat, poultry, fish and dairy produce and most sell eggs. Five million eggs are sold every year. Egg boxes are always brand new, never recycled and, to prevent conflicting standards, eggs are sold only by price. From July 2005 each egg must be stamped, in food-grade ink, with a 'Producer's code' issued by DEFRA, giving the establishment, country of origin and method of production. Producers of meat, poultry, fish or dairy products are as strictly controlled, and must also be registered with their local authority and their premises approved. If they are producing under organic or free-range conditions then the mind-numbing paperwork must be done, approved, licensed, updated annually, and made available to anyone.

The WI Hall, Bridport, Dorset

Egg Producing

Martin, Sue and George Weaver (see right and below right) have been supplying their local market at Chew Valley with eggs and garden produce every Friday since 2000. They have 300-400 hens which they only keep until 70 weeks old. This preserves the quality and the quantity of the eggs, providing enough to supply six markets in all.

Lindsey French (above) has been a part of the market since she was born. She now helps out in her holidays selling the eggs. "I enjoy seeing all my friends and I can choose which stall I sell on, but I like the eggs because its only me on my own, no grown ups!" Her grandmother, Joan Greenman was a founder member of Chew Valley Market, and still does the accounts.

Sue (left and above) helps sell at Chew Valley and five other farmer's markets in their region. She also does all the deliveries, rain or shine, donning an apron just in time to take the money.

Martin Weaver, egg producer and market gardener, with his son George and their Ida Brown Hens

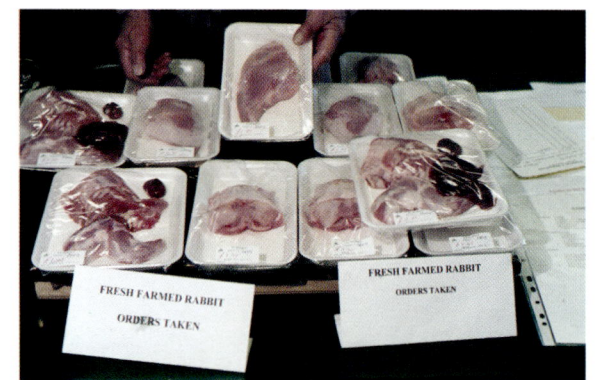

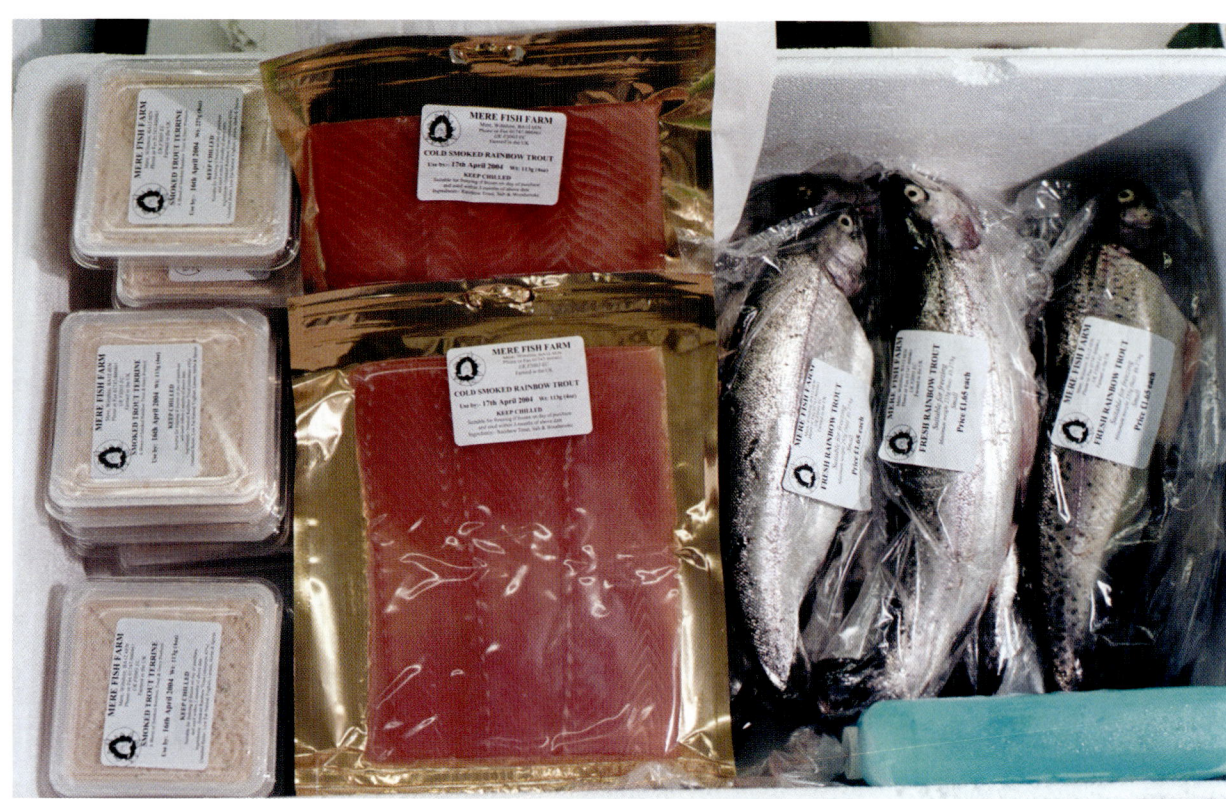

Clockwise from bottom left:
Sherborne, Shaftesbury, Shaftesbury

The Town Hall, Wadebridge, Cornwall

Beekeeping

Cyril and Barbara Smallwood [below] make a range of products for Cheltenham market from their bee's honey. They also attend their local Farmer's Market twice a month. Cyril belongs to the Association of Beekeepers. He uses the European Honey Bee [Apismellifera], the only bee indigenous to Britain, and the best for pollinating. He has tried Queen bees from New Zealand but found them less successful.

Derek Pont, above, has been beekeeping since he was eleven, first helping his father with the puffer. His bees feed on borage early in the year, and, later, on wild flowers and clover. *"They can get niggly! Especially if you cross their path when they're foraging."* Each hive produces about twice what the bees need to get them through the winter." Derek stockpiles the surplus to get through the same period. He sells honey and candles at Lincoln Market all year round. *"When you go out there of an evening, and you hear them all quietly humming in the hives, that is lovely really."*

Llew Patch, retired pharmacist, Ulverston, Cumbria

Organic Meat

Lower Failand farm produces organic beef and lamb for the North Somerset WI markets. All the animals are born and reared on the farm, only leaving it at the time of slaughter. The beef animals are an Aberdeen-Angus and South Devon cross. After supplying local markets, any surplus beef goes to a local Sainsbury's. The lamb, however, goes only to a Farmers' Market, the WI Markets and other local village markets. Mike Amos does all the finished butchering himself (see label, bottom right), and his son, Paul, helps with the ground work and tractor driving.

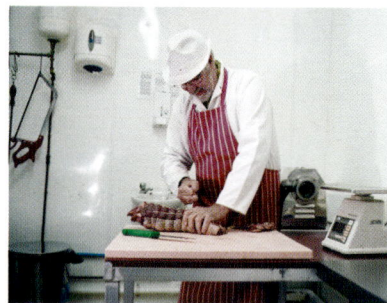

The farm also produces seasonal organic vegetables and fruit. Mike's wife, Carole, wraps and labels all the fruit and vegetables, as well as baking meat pies for the markets. The top fruit orchards (bottom centre) contain some traditional apple varieties such as Devonshire Quarrenden and Merchant of Ilminster and provide perfect grazing for the farm's Polled Dorset sheep.

Reference number 8/7/3UK361885/700067
Born reared & produced from
UK Lower Failand Organic Farm
Topside Price: £
Weight:
Slaughtered in : UK abattoir Bakers number 8149
Cut in. Lower Failand Organic Farm Cutting Room, @ Lower Failand Organic Farm, Bristol

Mike Amos, with his South Devon pedigree bull, George, at Lower Failand Organic Farm

9. The Cafés

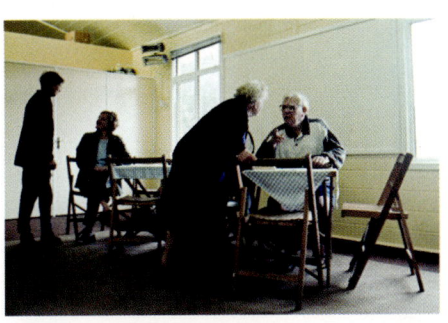

Clockwise from left:
Lincoln, Chew Valley, Guernsey, Clitheroe

Nearly sixty percent of the 500 markets operate a café of some kind. Between them, they serve 10,500 cups of tea and coffee each week, and at about 30p a cup this often includes a traditional home-baked biscuit and some local gossip. In each market every helper and producer takes turns for the weekly café duties of organising the supplies, serving, setting up the tables, clearing away and washing up.

78

Clockwise from bottom left:
Wool, Chapel St Leonards, Guernsey Vale, Harleston, Pwllheli

The Old Barn Hall, Great Bookham, Surrey

The WI Hall, Harleston, Norfolk

10. The Orders

Clockwise from left:
Great Bookham, Greet, Clitheroe, Isle of Portland

Orders can be given by phone, email or in person at the weekly market. Almost every market dedicates at least one table for items ordered in advance – an often necessary precaution against the locust-style 'queue'. As well as individual items the WI Market Parcel Scheme is open to anyone. A box of goodies can be ordered at one branch and delivered locally, in person, by another, or the head office in Chesterfield will pass orders on. Up to 3,000 parcels are delivered each year; many are sent to the elderly who can no longer get to the market, to students living away from home, or to someone who deserves a treat.

The Pensioners' Hall, Llantwit Major, Vale of Glamorgan

11. The Venues

Clockwise from top left:
Cheltenham, Hertford, Charing, Buxton

Village halls, church halls and scout huts, theatres and corn exchanges, restored barns and stables, old schools and railway stations, farmer's markets and street markets, town halls, guildhalls, libraries, pubs and labour clubs, sports and community centres, front rooms, market squares and car parks. Salisbury market's caravan is towed into place in the Guildhall square car park each Saturday at 6am and towed away again at 4pm. *"None of us can remember what we used to do on Saturdays!"*

pages 86-87: The Guildhall Square, Salisbury, Wiltshire

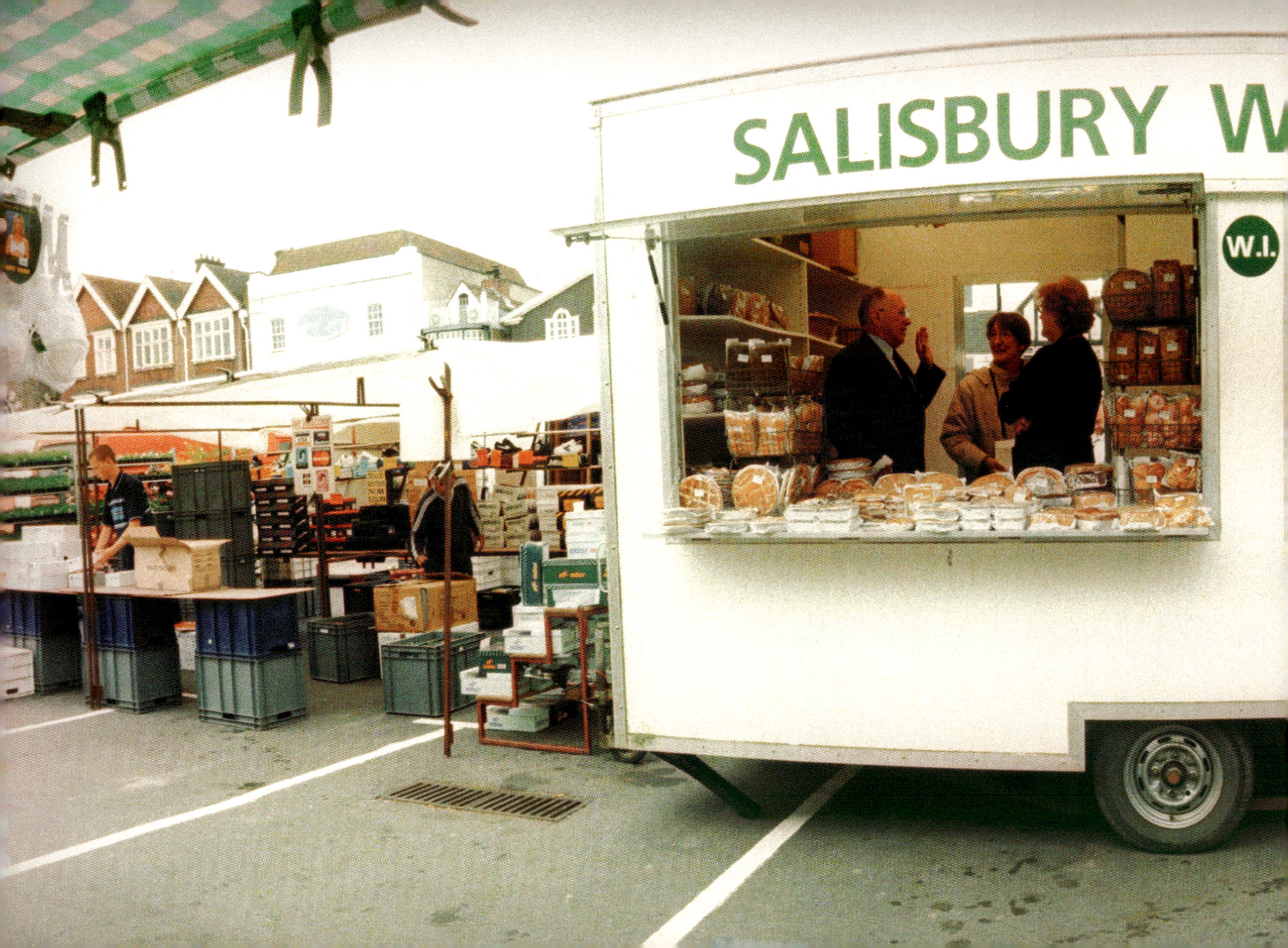
SALISBURY
W.I.

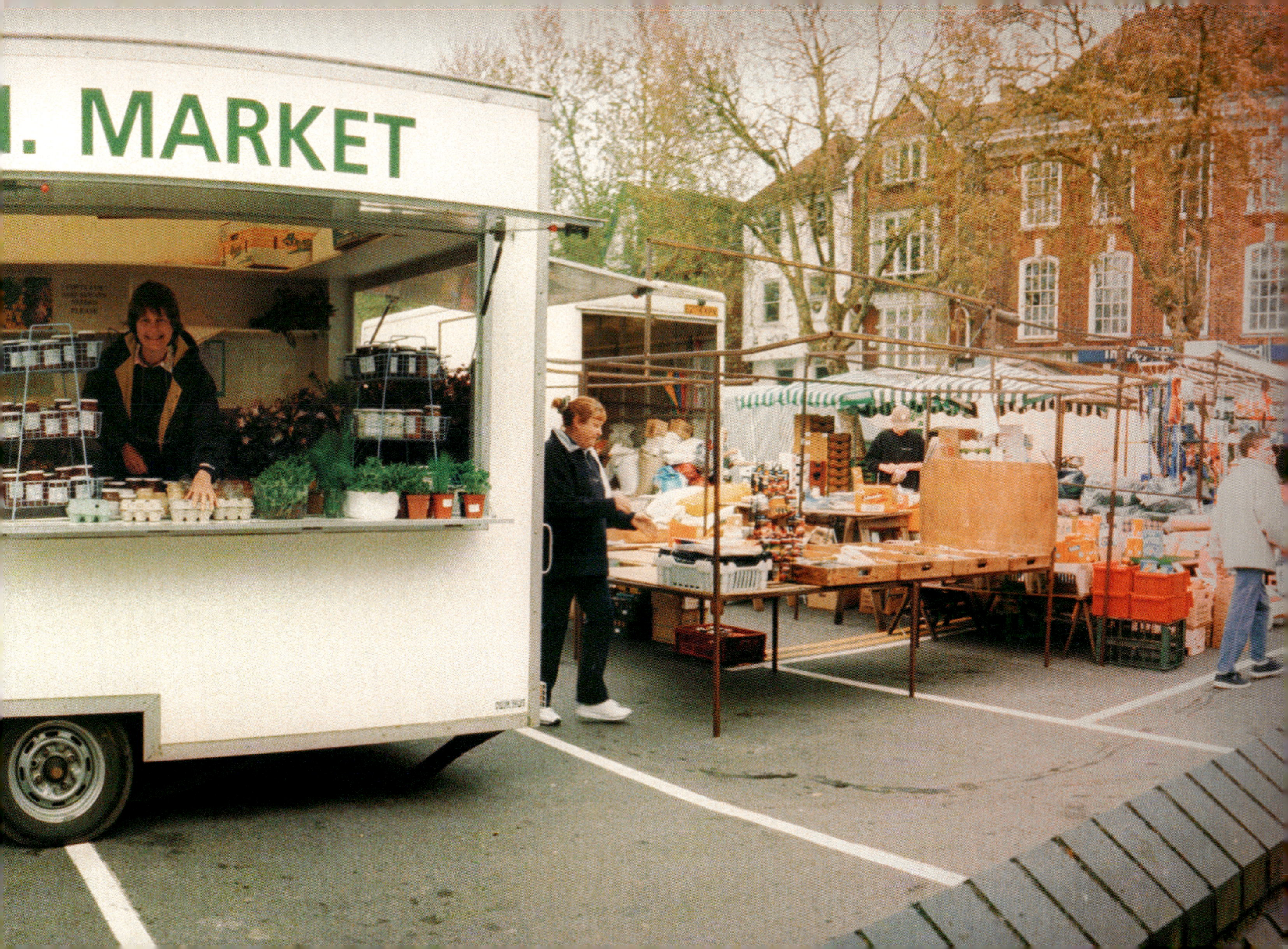

MARKET

Left to right from top left: Pwllheli, Hertford, Backwell, Leominster, Pwllheli, Sleaford. Bottom right: Melton Mowbray

Left to right from top: Clitheroe, Ulverston, Greet, Knighton, Yateley, Charing, Ludlow

12. The Helpers

The Town Hall, Launceston, Cornwall

On average each of the 500 markets has 10-15 helpers, and many of these are producers as well. But nearly every market can sport a helper or two who come along, either for the fun of it or out of a real desire to help. And a lot of help is needed: setting up tables, sorting tablecloths, getting money from the bank (for change), helping with the check-in of produce, sorting the refreshments (for customers or workers, or both), putting up (sometimes even making) the advertisement sign outside, putting up rotas, manning the stalls, taking the money, and then dismantling it all when it's over. Good helpers, the unsung heroes of the markets, are often the first to arrive, the last to leave, and don't get paid a penny for it.

Left to right from top: Lincon, Stokesley, Leominster, Conway, Sherborne, Lincoln, Llangefni, Clitheroe

Left to right from top: Guernsey Vale, Harleston, Marshalswick, Guernsey Vale, Pwllheli, Ware, Chew Valley, Wool. Bottom right: Chichester

93

13. The Customers

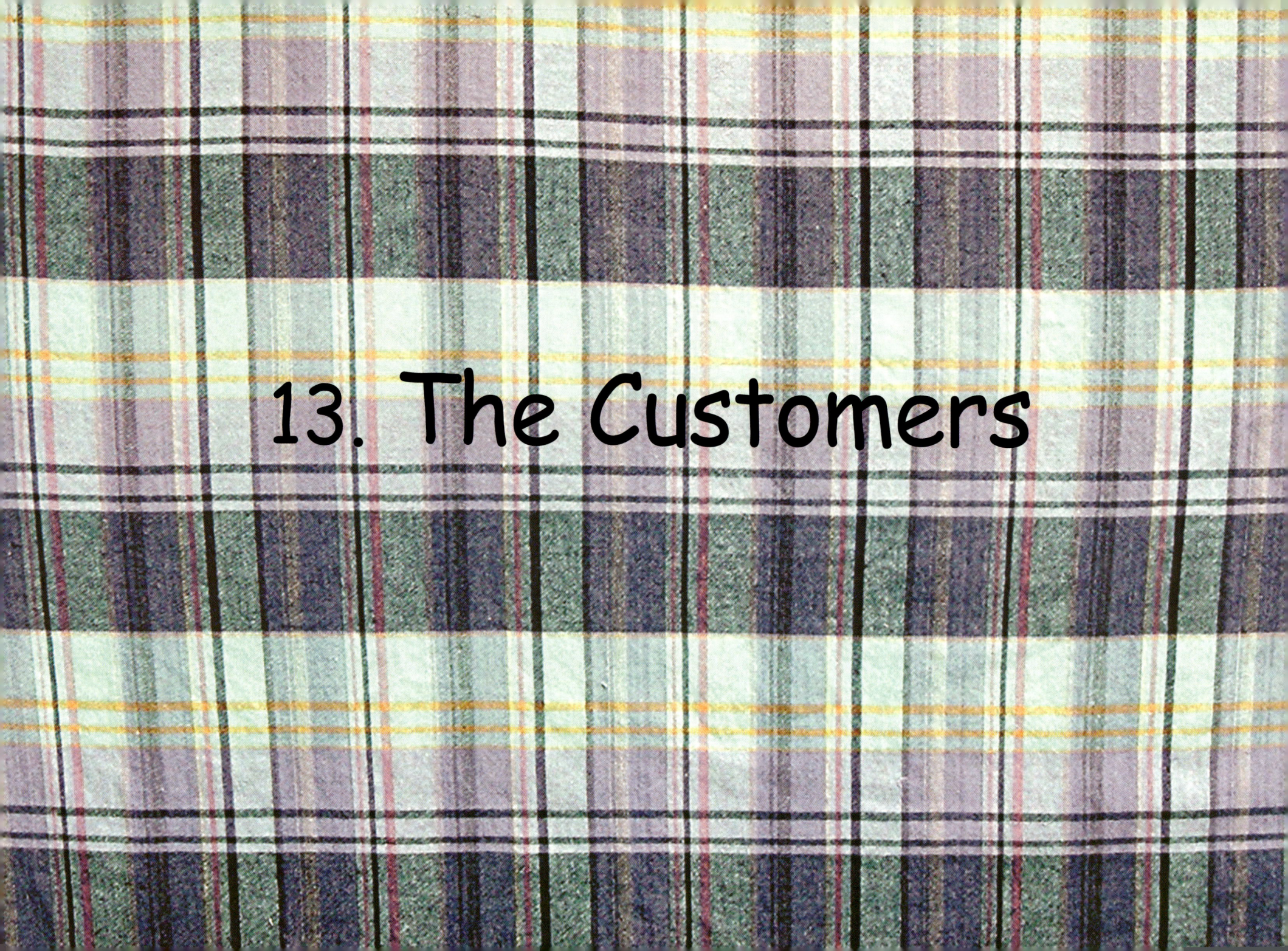

The Parish Rooms, Newport, Shropshire

Tourists, grandads, young mums and students, council workers and policeman out buying their lunch; friends shopping together; housewives shopping for families; dads seeking Christmas presents; mums seeking any presents; children shopping for mums; gardeners looking for plants; pensioners looking for bargains; shoppers queuing, bustling, browsing; rows of shoppers, groups of shoppers, solitary shoppers and gossipy shoppers; early shoppers and choosy shoppers, . . . and each of them carrying a purse.

Left to right from top: Chew Magna, Ludlow, Shaftesbury, Clitheroe, Kirkby Lonsdale, Swanage, Chapel St Leonard's, Charing, Chew Valley, Conway

Left to right from top: Barnard Castle, Dorchester, Ludlow, Lincoln, Harleston, Salisbury, Marshalswick, Newick, Lindfield, Guernsey Vale, Melton Mowbray, Backwell, Clitheroe

14. The Economics

The Town Hall, Northallerton, North Yorkshire

Playing shops with £11 million a year

Around ten percent of this turnover covers administration costs, the remainder is returned to the individual producer, who get involved, not just for this profit but for the love of cooking, gardening or making things. Of the 44,000 shareholders, only 13,000 are producers. The rest do it for fun. *"We have a great time, we all get together and once a week we get to play shops"*

The £11 million turnover: where does it come from?

Throughout the country, WI Markets take place at least 24,000 times a year. At the time of writing the average turnover of each of the 500 branches is £22,000 a year (£458 per week). The sums quickly add up. The average number of producers per branch is 26. This means that each producer produces around £850 worth of produce per year. For a cake producer, selling a cake at £2.50, this represents 7 cakes each week. To compare £11 million a year with seven home-made cakes a week goes some way towards understanding the extremes of scale within the WI Markets organisation throughout the United Kingdom.

Some producers, of course, generate more than a handful of cakes a week, and many produce fewer. But no producer can sell anywhere unless there is a customer ready and waiting. Similarly, a producer will not waste time dragging goods to market, week in, week out, if no one is going to buy them; not even for their free tea and biscuits and a good gossip. (There may, of course, be quite a few who do exactly that!) Nearly all producers will be prepared to take some of their produce back home with them, and a shrewd producer will always have ready a little more than was sold the previous week. In this way, the supply almost perfectly matches local demand, and the widespread patronage ensures that the turnover, across the country, is reliably sustained.

Where does the money go?

A hypothetical shareholder, whom I shall call Jane, will join a market by paying 5p to the County Market Society. This share capital is held in a separate society bank account. (It is not included in the trading figures.) But Jane will also pay out approximately £6 for The Handbook which gives her step-by-step guidance both on how to produce and how to run a market. Her £6 goes to the limited company. Let's say that Jane then bakes a cake. The cost of the ingredients (say £1) is doubled and 25% is added to this sum; this gives a selling price of £2.50 for Jane's cake. When the cake is sold at market the branch banks the money. One month later, after taking the branch commission (usually 10%), Jane is paid back £2.25. The 25p commission is mostly retained in the branch bank account to help cover the rent for the venue and any of the branch committee expenses. Also, out of Jane's 25p, a small amount is paid, quarterly, to the county society as a subscription. This, the money for the handbooks and any contributing sponsorship from outside, is all that the organisation can generate to fund itself; to run a head office with two employees and a board of directors; to produce audits, cover insurance and to hold an AGM; to train market advisers; to produce a quarterly magazine; to run the web site; and to send, when necessary, a representative to Parliament, to the European Commission or to anyone else with a mind to interfere.

What makes a successful market?

Location, location, location doesn't just apply to buying and selling homes. It is also the strongest asset or the weakest point for a WI Market. For instance, Harleston in South Norfolk marketed merrily enough for six years in the old Women's Institute's hall tucked away behind a pub. But when forced to move out the Market was faced with the dilemma of using the new leisure centre, even further from the centre of the village, or squeezing into the main village hall only a few steps from the market square itself. Imagine their delight, when, having decided to trim their space so drastically at the village hall, their turnover shot up by 20%! Wellingborough Market, on the other hand, has had to face the opposite problem. Since the supermarket next door (a name we all know and hate) claimed rights over the car park, denying cheap all day parking for the townsfolk, their weekly takings dropped by a third. (The ensuing bitterness between this David and Goliath included the mysterious disappearance of the WI Market sign!) Efforts to find a good alternative location in the town came to nothing, and Wellingborough Market has now closed. In this instance, the blindness of the supermarket to the welfare of the community won the day, and this local amenity has now gone, perhaps forever. (Come on, Wellingborough! There must be somewhere else in a town with a population of over 70,000.

Is there an un-successful market?

A market's success is, superficially, measured by how much money it generates. But even the smallest Market still makes a profit for its producers, however few there may be. Someone at home enjoying Jane's cake is one happy customer, and Jane still gets some profit from the £2.25. But for a visitor, it is the ambience of a market that counts. The atmosphere can encourage you to linger and spend, or have you charging for the exit as soon as you've picked up your change. If the market is upbeat it will have a party atmosphere; the feeling that this is an 'event'. It will be a more progressive market; more forward-looking than some and is more likely to begin with a noisy queue. It will generate more producers and may even encourage a new branch within the county. But some markets are downbeat. They are quieter. The people involved will often have a strong sense of the past and may even be a little backward-looking to the pre-supermarket years when their particular market had many more customers and producers each week. But this is not to say that their market is not a success and that it has no part to play in the whole story, because it does. Whatever kind of market, and there are many that fall between these two extremes, nobody makes a loss that they cannot sustain. The customers get as much or as little as they need. All markets have their own loyal following and in this they are all playing a valuable part in their community. No matter how much momentum is lost by one branch as it winds down over a period of years, there will be another in the county gaining in momentum. In this way The growth of the WI Markets is self-renewing and organic, and can only get stronger over the years. These fluctuations are their strength, and such diverse economic platforms within the corporate structure are their secret. This, and their individual and collective commitment, results in a flexible yet unbreakable bond between economic success, community welfare and personal fulfillment.

(Figures are based on 46 trading weeks as very few markets operate during January or through the Christmas period.)

15. The Future

A new name for a new century

Whilst talking recently, once again, to Judy Forbes at Harleston, whom I mentioned in the Introduction, I was struck by a certain lack of confidence on her part in the market's overall future. And yet with almost the same breath she expressed a feeling shared by many other shareholders. "We really are a sister- and brotherhood. Wherever we go in the country, on holiday for instance, we visit the local market and feel a part of it." So many people all wanting to share the same thing are not simply going to disappear overnight. So how do you explain this apparent conflict between feeling no confidence in the future, and the – equally strong – belief in the strength and unity of the Markets? The answer is that many of the people involved can only view the markets on a purely practical level, not taking on board the deeper, longer lasting issues, surrounding their enterprise. In the face of supermarket retailing they feel threatened.

They only see, for instance, their own small market, or a few within the surrounding area. It's not that they feel isolated; they just don't have a clue what the rest of the 500 markets are getting up to. The everyday workings of the organisation as a whole are quite disparate; this is built into the structure. For one marketeer to view another market is the exception, not the rule. In short they don't know their own strength.

Many express a fear that their average age group is working against them, when in reality it is only a more mature group who can, and want, to give their time so generously: a group whose numbers are swelling, year upon year. It is true that among the active players (but not the customers, it must be said) the under 40s are few and far between. Younger, more energetic, people with grand ideas of how the world should work might view the markets with a certain amount of derision, particularly if they are city dwellers. But this is no knitting B that we are talking about, nor just a sewing circle that happens to bake a bit on the side. This is a national organisation, a network of activity that reaches from the Channel Islands to Northumberland, from East Anglia to Anglesey. These are 44,000 people who can speak with one voice when they need to, who are able and willing to contribute to the needs of their home communities, often as nothing more than volunteers, and all with the weight of corporate power behind them, whatever their age. With their new name, a name that will grow into a new identity, anything could now happen. Their future has never looked stronger.

Offering an overall view I hope that this book will help bring with it a new confidence within the markets themselves. It may even inspire someone to become involved whose values include shared experience, practical activity and a nice bit of home-made cake. The Country Markets, as they are now known, are there for everyone.

What do you need to start a new market? Time – loads of it. A few good friends willing to be re-defined as your steering committee. Producers – as many as you can trawl in. A good site. The handbook. There's a lot more to it than this, but this is a start. What you don't need is masses of money, hundreds of producers (Fakenham has three), acres of room (Wincanton operate in someone's front room) nor do you necessarily need to be female or a member of the National Federation of Women's Institutes.

What do you do first? Call the Country Market's head office in Chesterfield (01246 261508). Hold an open meeting to bash ideas around, e.g. when and where to hold the market. Pick the brains of the County Market Adviser. You need to find out about regulations, packaging, procedure. Elect your committee and officers. Submit your proposal to the county society to become shareholders. Pay your 5p!

PUBLICISE everywhere! Local press and radio, hand out leaflets, pin a note to a friendly tree. Have another meeting for producers and helpers. Buy, borrow or make necessary equipment you will need; tablecloths, tables, display stands, etc. The Country Market's corporate image is an asset – use it.

Clockwise from top left: Felixstowe, Harleston, Harleston

What then? Some legal work is needed: affiliate to the county society and open a bank account. The handbook from head office gives step by step guidance on this less exciting part of the process. Elect a controller – the backbone of the market. The Controllers' most important function is quality control. With the greatest amount of diplomacy their word is law. They are the merchandisers, pricing gurus and settlers of disputes. The smooth running of the market depends on how well they do these difficult tasks. They are selected by secret ballot. In markets of more than just a few people a frisson of excitement usually surrounds the election of the controller. If this happens then you know that you are all hooked.

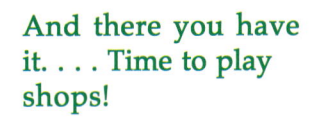

And there you have it. . . . Time to play shops!

Whether you bake, make, preserve, grow, organise or simply help with the tea, you are probably saying goodbye to your spare time. Your Christmas card list will most likely double in length and you will never again be able to walk the length of your high street un-accosted by new friends. But don't worry, neither you nor your community, and certainly not your ageing mother if you have one (who will be able to add one more summer outing to her list) are likely to regret it.

Clockwise from left: Guernsey Vale, Aylsham, Charing,

16. The Facts and the Directory

General statistics

Markets: 480
Shareholders: 44,000
County societies: 81
Producers, approximately: 13,000
Helpers, approximately: 7,000

Product statistics per year

(Approximate, figures taken from surveys carried out in 2001 & 2002)

Bread loaves: 340,000
Large cakes: 886,000
Small food items: 1.8 million
Savouries: 1.9 million

Flour: 888,000 kilos
Fat: 533,000 kilos
Sugar: 380,000

Jars of preserves: 790,000
Jars of honey: 85,000
Eggs: 5 million

Vegetables: 250,000 kilos
Vegetable plants: 620,000
Potted plants: 880,000
Cut flowers: 165,000 bunches

Craft items: 200,000

Refreshment venues: 356
Cups of tea & coffee: 10,500

Annual turnovers

1916-1991: Unknown
1992: £10,600,000
1993: £10,360,000
1994: £10,800,000
1995: £10,800,000
1996: £11,200,000
1997: £10,800,000
1998: £11,100,000
1999: £11,000,000
2000: £10,800,000
2001: £10,930,000
2002: £10,900,000
2003: £10,900,000
2004: £10,950,000

Chronology

1897: First institute formed in Stoney Creek, Ontario, Canada
1915: First institute in Britain in Llanfair PG on Anglesey
1916: First market in Criccieth, Caernarfon
1917: Lewes Market opened (still trading)
1920: Guild of Learners formed to promote home crafts
1922: Crafts exhibition at the Victoria & Albert Museum in London
1932: Carnegie UK Trust grant enables markets to begin trading separately from the National Federation of Women's Institutes
1939: Produce guild formed to encourage home produce
1940: First grant from the Ministry of Food
1940: Co-operative Fruit Preservation Scheme funded by Ministry of Agriculture
1947: Operation Produce launched
1962-66: Freedom from Hunger Campaign
1972: Home economics courses begin, replacing both Produce and Handicrafts Guilds
1995: Markets begin trading as a limited, non-profit-making company, WI Markets Limited
2004: WI Markets Ltd change its name to Country Markets Limited

Further reading

Davies, Constance: *A grain of mustard seed*, Gee & Son, Denbigh, 2nd ed., 1989
Goodenough, Simon: *Jam & Jerusalem*, Collins, Glasgow & London, 1977
Goodenough, Simon: *The greatest good fortune, a history of the Carnegie Trusts*, Macdonald Publishers, Edinburgh, 1985
Jenkins, Ivey: *The history of the Women's Institute movement in England & Wales*, OUP, 1953
Drage, Dorothy: *Pennies for friendship*, Private. 1961
Dudgeon, Piers: *Village voices*, WI Books Ltd., 1989
Robertson, Scott: *The story of the Women's Institute movement in England, Wales and Scotland*, Village Press, Idbury, 1925

Internet connections

www.country-markets.co.uk
www.womensinstitute.org.uk
www.cooponline.co.uk
www.farmersmarkets.net

The Directory

For the dates, times and specific locations of markets contact Country Markets Ltd: 01246 261508

Avon Backwell, Bath, Bristol, Chew Magna, Chipping Sodbury, Clevedon, Doynton, Keynsham, Marshfield, Nailsea, Portishead, Westbury, Weston-super-Mare, Wrington Vale

Bedfordshire Ampthill, Bedford, Dunstable, Shefford

Berkshire Cookham, Earley, Pangbourne, Reading, Tadley, Thatcham, Wokingham, Yateley

Buckinghamshire Amersham, Buckingham, Milton Keynes, Olney, Princes Risborough, Thame

Cambridgeshire Cambridge, Great Shelford

Carmarthenshire Carmarthen, Llandeilo, Llandovery, Llanelli, Newcastle Emlyn

Ceredigion Aberaeron, Aberporth, Aberystwyth, Cardigan, Lampeter, New Quay, Tregaron

Cheshire Farndon, Frodsham, Macclesfield, Nantwich, Neston, Tattenhall, Willaston on Wirral

Clwd-Denbighshire Denbigh, Glan Conwy, Llangollen, Ruthin, Wrexham

Clwyd-Flintshire Harwarden, Mold

Cornwall Callington, Helston, Illogan, Launceston, Liskeard, Penzance, Perranporth, Porstcatho, Torpoint, Veryan, Wadebridge

Cumbria Ambleside, Brampton, Cockermouth, Appleby, Kirby Lonsdale, Milnthorpe, Penrith, Ulverston, Whitehaven, Wigton

Derbyshire Bakewell Buxton, Chesterfield, Derby, Hathersage, Matlock

Devon Axminster Barnstaple, Bideford, Exeter, Exmouth, Holsworthy, Honiton, Ivybridge, Kingsbridge, South Molton, Tavistock, Tiverton

Dorset Bridport, Christchurch, Dorchester, Gillingham, Isle of Portland, Kinson, Shaftesbury, Sherborne, Sturminster Newton, Swanage, Verwood, Wimborne, Wool

Durham Barnard Castle, Darlington, Lanchester, Sedgefield

Essex Bishop's Stortford, Danbury, Great Dunmow, Halstead, Hatfield Peverel, Maldon, Rayleigh, Saffron Waldon, Shenfield, Walton

Glamorgan Cowbridge, Llantwit Major, Oystermouth, Porthcawl

Gloucestershire Cheltenham Chipping Campden, Cirencester, Coleford, Fairford, Gloucester, Lechlade, Minchinhampton, Moreton-in-Marsh, Nailsworth, Newent, Northleach, Painswick, Stroud, Tewkesbury, Winchcombe

Guernsey St Peters, Guernsey Vale

Gwent Chepstow, Monmouth, Newport, Usk

Gwynedd-Caernarfon Conwy, Dolgellau, Pwllheli, Trefriw

Gwynedd-Isle of Anglesey Llangefni

Hampshire Alresford, Alton, Andover, Bishops Waltham, Fareham, Fordingbridge, Hartley-Wintney, Hythe, Romsey, Stubbington, Titchfield, Winchester

Herefordshire Bromyard, Hereford, Kington, Ledbury, Leominster, Ross-on-Wye

Hertfordshire Baldock, Berkhamptead, Bovingdon, Harpenden, Hatfield, Hertford, Kings Langley, Marshalswick, Royston, St Albans, Sawbridgworth, Ware

Huntingdon Huntingdon, St Ives, St Neots

Isle of Wight Freshwater, Newport, Ryde, Shanklin, Yarmouth

Jersey St Helier

Kent Ashford, Bearstead, Bexley, Borough Green, Charing, Dover, East Peckham, Eynsford, Hawkshurst, Hythe, Ide Hill, Longfield, Maidstone, Orpington, Rochester, Romney Marsh, Sandwich, Sevenoaks, Sittingbourne, Tenterden, Thanet, Tonbridge, Tunbridge Wells, Wilmington
Lancashire Carnforth, Clitheroe, Garstang, Kirkham Longton
Leicestershire & Rutland Birstall, Blaby, Glenfield, Hinckley, Lutterworth, Market Harborough, Melton Mowbray, Oadby, Oakham, Syston
Lincolnshire Alford, Gainsborough, Grantham, Lincoln, Market Rasen, Sleaford, Stamford, Wainfleet, Woodhall Spa
London Barnes
Middlesex Ruislip
Norfolk Aylesham, Brooke, Dereham, Diss, Downham Market, Drayton, Fakenham, Harleston, Heacham, Holt, Kings Lynn, Loddon, North Walsham, Reepham, Sheringham, Swaffham, Watton, Wisbech, Wymondham
Northamptonshire Brackley, Daventry, Long Buckby, Oundle, Towcester
Northumberland Hexham, Morpeth, Ponteland
North Yorkshire Easingwold, Northallerton, Otley, Pickering, Selby, Stockton, Stokesley, York
Nottinghamshire Bingham, Mansfield, Newark, Nottingham, Retford, Southwell, Worksop
Oxfordshire Abingdon, Banbury, Bicester, Bloxham, Burford, Chipping Norton, Eynsham, Faringdon, Henley-on-Thames, Wallingford, Wantage, Witney
Pembrokeshire Fishguard, Haverfordwest, Manorbier, Narberth, Pembroke, Penally, Saundersfoot, St Davids, Tenby
Powys – Montgomeryshire Newton, Welshpool
Powys – Radnor/Brecknock Brecon, Bulith Wells, Hay-on-Wye, Knighton, Llandrindod Wells
Shropshire Bridgenorth, Church Stretton, Ludlow, Market Drayton, Much Wenlock, Newport, Oswestry, Shrewsbury, Wellington, Whitchurch
Somerset Bridgewater, Chard ,Cheddar, Crewkerne, Frome, Glastonbury, Langport, Minehead, Somerton, Street, Taunton, Wells, Williton, Wincanton, Yeovil
South Yorkshire Doncaster, Holmfirth, Penistone, Sheffield, Tickhill
Staffordshire Brewood, Burton, Codshall, Eccleshall, Leek, Morlands, Lichfield, Newcastle-under-Lyme, Rugeley, Stafford, Stone, Tamworth, Uttoxeter
Suffolk Beccles, Bungay, Bury St Edmunds, Clare, Eye, Felixstowe, Framlingham, Hadleigh, Halesworth, Ipswich, Long Melford, Lowestoft, Martlesham Heath, Newmarket, Southwold, Stowmarket, Woodbridge
Surrey Banstead, Bookham, Chobham, Cranleigh, Dorking, Redhill, Elmbridge, Farnham, Godalming, Guildford, Horley, Leatherhead, Oxted, Richmond, Windlesham, Woking
Sussex Ardingly, Arundel, Battle, Burgess Hill, Chichester, Crowborough, Durrington, Emsworth, Felpham, Ferring, Hastings, Havant, Lancing, Lewes, Lindfield, Mayfield, Newhaven, Newick, Petworth, Pevensey Bay, Ringmer, Rustington, Rye, Selsey, Southwick, Storrington, West Worthing, Waldron
Tyne and Wear Washington, Durham, Ryton, Whitley Bay, Tynemouth
Warwickshire Alcester, Colehill, Leamington Spa, Rugby, Shipston-on-Stour, Stratford-upon-Avon
West Midlands Allesley, Balshall Common, Dorridge
Wiltshire Amesbury, Bradford-on-Avon, Chippenham, Corsham, Cricklade, Devizes, Downton, Pewsey, Salisbury, Swindon, Tisbury, Warminster, Westbury, Wilton, Wroughton
Worcestershire Droitwich, Evesham, Hagley, Malvern, Pershore, Tenbury, Wells, Worcester
Yorkshire East Beverley

Index

AGM, Westminster City Hall 2001, 14
Amos, Mike, Carole & Paul, 74-75
AOS (Agricultural Organisations Society), 9
Aylsham, Norfolk, 105

Backwell, North Somerset, 46, 88, 97
Barnard Castle, Durham, 60, 97
Brampton, Cumbria, 12
Bridport, Dorset, 33, 67
Burgess, Barbara, 62-63
Buxton, Derbyshire, 85

Carnegie UK Trust, 10
Chapel St Leonards, Lincolnshire, 46, 78, 96
Charing, Kent, 56, 85, 89, 96, 105
Cheltenham, Gloucestershire, 85
Chew Valley, Avon, 46, 68, 77, 93. 96
Chichester, Hampshire, 93, 13
Clitheroe, Lancashire, 55, 58, 61, 77, 82, 89, 92,96,97
Conway, Caernarfon, 55, 62, 92, 96
Country Markets Head Office, Chesterfield, 104, 108
Country Markets Ltd., 16
County societies, 16
Cowbridge, Vale of Glamorgan, 19
Craner, Pam, 50-51
Criccieth, Caernarfon, 11

DEFRA (Department for Environment, Food and Rural Affairs), 42
Denman College, 36
Dorchester, Dorset, 55, 97
Drage, Dorothy, 9, 11
Droitwich, Worcestershire, 22, 32

Eden Valley, Cumbria, 20, 22, 32,34
Evesham, Worcestershire, 20, 32

Fakenham, Norfolk, 104
Felixstowe, Suffolk 104
Forbes, Judy, 5, 103
French, Lindsay, 68
FSA (Financial Services Act), 16

Giles, Michelle, 60
Graham, Jill, 24
Great Bookham, Surrey, 79, 82
Greet, Gloucestershire, 32, 56,60, 82, 89
Guernsey Vale, Guernsey, 64, 77, 78, 93, 97, 105

Handbook 1932, 10
Harleston, Norfolk, 5, 38, 47, 78, 80, 93, 97, 100, 103, 104
Helston, Cornwall, 44-45
Hertford, Hertfordshire, 85, 88
Hexham, Northumberland, 40
Holsworthy, Devon, 12, 21

ICA (Independent Co-operative Association), 10
Isle of Portland, Dorset, 26, 46, 55, 82
Jones, Audrey, 24
Kirkby Lonsdale, Cumbria, 96
Knight, Peggy, 26-27
Knighton, Radnor, 89

Launceston, Cornwall, 91
Leach, Derek, 61
Leominster, Herefordshire, 88, 92
Lewes, East Sussex, 8, 9
Lincoln, Lincolnshire, 20,32, 72, 77, 92, 97
Lindfield, East Sussex, 97
Llanfair, Isle of Anglesey, 11
Llangefni, Isle of Anglesey, 24, 92
Llantwit Major, Glamorgan, 83
Locke. Bill, 60
Long Melford, Suffolk, 43
Lower Failand farm, Somerset 74-75
Ludlow, Shropshire, 22, 56, 59, 60, 89, 96, 97
Lush, Ray, 36-37

Marks, Diane, 60
Marshalswick, Hertfordshire, 32, 58, 93, 97
Melton Mowbray, Leicestershire, 22, 88, 97
Moreton-in-Marsh, Gloucestershire, 24
Moss, Charles, 49

Newick, East Sussex, 97
Newport, Shropshire, 95
NFWI (National Federation of Women's Institutes), 5, 6, 8, 10, 16, 104
Norris, Bridget, 36-37
Northallerton, North Yorkshire, 53, 99

Patch, Lew, 73
Paul, Hilary, 48
Pont, Derek, 72
Princes Risborough, Buckinghamshire, 12
Pwllheli, Caernarfon, 12, 78, 88, 93,

Roseland, Cornwall, 56, 57
Ruislip, Middlesex, 29

Salisbury, Wiltshire, 86-87, 97
Shaftesbury, Dorset, 70, 96
Sherborne, Dorset, 56, 70, 92
Sleaford, Lincolnshire, 88
Smallwood, Barbara & Cyril, 72
St Helier, Jersey, 48, 55
Stevenson, John, 49
Stokesley, North Yorkshire, 23, 92
Stoney Creek, Ontario, 8
Swanage, Dorset, 96

Thomas, Hilda, 38-39
Thwaytes, Fiona, 34-35

Trefriw, Caernarfon, 62

Ulverston, Cumbria, 73, 89

Wadebridge, Cornwall, 71
Ware, Hertfordshire, 58, 93
Watt, Mrs Alfred, 8
Weaver, Martin, Sue & George, 68-69
Wellingborough, Northamptonshire, 100
Whitley Bay, Tyne & Wear, 14, 31
Wincanton, Somerset, 104
Wool, Dorset, 22, 78, 93

Yateley, Hampshire, 20, 36-37, 89

With thanks to:

the people of the W.I. Markets, especially to Harleston; to Anne Stamper, Honorary Archivist to NFWI and to Pat Green of Milton Keynes for her valuable find; to Peter K, Peter V, and Peter W, and to Keith and my lovely Mum, and to my unfailing co-driver, sub-editor and lighting expert, Brian.
Thanks also to Flash PhotoDigital.